THE WAY IT WAS

The Way It Was

POEMS BY
LEONARD CLARK

THE ENITHARMON PRESS
1980

First published in 1980
by The Enitharmon Press
22 Huntingdon Road,
East Finchley, London N2 9DU

© Leonard Clark 1980

ISBN 0 905289 12 9 (wrappers)
ISBN 0 905289 17 X (hardbound)

The Enitharmon Press
acknowledges financial assistance from
the Arts Council of Great Britain

*Printed and made in Great Britain
by Skelton's Press, Wellingborough, Northants*

CONTENTS

Green Man Wandering	7
Easter	8
From A Hill	8
Rehearsal	10
Voices	12
The Hill	14
The Wheat	15
Country Funeral	16
Hawthorn	17
Village Idiot	18
Landscape	19
The Swans	20
Prisoner	21
Elements	22
Zero Hour	23
Mystical	24
Neutrality	25
Water Meadows	26
Flowers for Winter	27
The Valley	28
Victims	29
Terror	30
Sedgemoor	31
Marsh	32
Birdlip Mirror	34
Cider-House	36
On the Border	38
Biological Experiment	40
Delivery	41
Still Born	42
Deaf and Dumb	43
Mongol	44
The Births	45
Master of the Choristers	46
Late of This Parish	48
Visit to Edmund Blunden	49
For a Christening	50

Early Portrait	51
Maurice	52
Rector	53
Virger	54
Retrospect of Andrew Young	55
Listening and Travelling	56
Sermons in Stones	57
Stedman	58
Nothing Lost	59
Bellringers	60
Sunday	61
No Ringer	63
Fathom Five	65
Scaleber Beck	66
Silences	67
Exiles	68
Valley of Shadow	69
The Way It Was	70
Vigil	71
The Sounding of the Horn	72
Christe, Christe	73
Benediction	74
Pilgrim	75
Prayer to God The Father	76

GREEN MAN WANDERING

A green man wandering all his days
with foxes running red in twilight
through frosted fern, deer standing motionless
in the moon's liquid eyes by antlered trees,
pin-point of a morning kestrel circling between hills;
wanders all seasons, all weathers.

Head bared to the wind's hammer he walks
in wondering silence the flowering land
of blackthorn breaking out of winter,
knots of primroses hunched under deep hedges,
floats with first royal butterfly,
swims the great drowning flood of bluebells.

Not crazed, but jubilant,
his ears are tuned to the cuckoo's clock,
eyes for flash of kingfisher, trout
imprisoned for a rainbow moment
between wimpling water and air.

He takes the frogged pools with him,
dragonflies and marsh marigolds,
into the daisied meadows of summer,
ploughs slowly on to harvest,
the whole earth ripening for him,
the heavens.

And when the larks rise to the sun,
singing the warm songs of apple trees,
he puts on the new clothes of the resurrection,
in a twinkling becomes a grass blade,
is mossed all over with immortality,
dances with scarecrows and shooting stars,
shares his secrets only with laughing bees.

A green man,
wandering.

EASTER

The woods come green again, the meadows waking,
Lambs charge at nothing on the hills,
And what a din the crazy rooks are making,
With April but a name for daffodils.

The lanes look primrose, the first blackthorn's showing,
Five spots of ladybird are going for a walk,
And here the ploughing's done, and there the barley's growing,
A drowsy mouse is nibbling at a stalk.

A shower of rain, three magpies for a wedding,
As now on Waddon's slope the shadows creep
And half across the sky a glorious rainbow spreading,
And only moles on Eggardon asleep.

FROM A HILL

Why from this particular hill
I am given to see through morning haze
A vision of the countryside
As it was in the olden days,
Dressed up for spring, unspoiled and still,
I cannot tell. But there it is, the land
Open to all, with acres stretching wide,
Curving up and down, spanned
Overhead by the huge arc of the sky.

From a farmhouse chimney, smoke
Curls freely into rain-washed air;
Across a field a man in corduroy
Guides a belled horse, a bright ploughshare,
The patterned furrows forming one by one;
He sings a song he learned as a boy
Of long-dead lovers walking in the sun.

Nibbling the young grass by a stream,
A flock of gently-crying sheep
Moves white as in a noontide dream,
Lambs run races, keen to leap
For joy of being just alive,
And in an orchard, pears and plums,
The blossoms powdering a squat straw hive
With bees humming like little drums.

I have had this vision once before,
A sudden moment in unfettered days
When young and standing at my cottage door
The happy world and I were all ablaze;
Love was speaking clearly to me then
As now it speaks, this season of the year,
The hedges coming new and quick again,
And you and I, in rapture, standing here.

REHEARSAL

The cycle of the year turns;
the winter spectacle reappears
with starved skies, skeleton trees,
sheep tugging away impassively at frozen roots
in desolate, stony fields
where songless birds have no shadows,
all creatures have gone underground.

The old drama of the seasons is played out again
against a backcloth of iron hills,
streams half-iced, silent,
the scenery only changing with the light
from chill dawn to chillier dusk.

Each element in this familiar landscape
knows its part, no effort needed
to remember the lines, how the plot goes;
the play will have the same ending,
reach the same inevitable climax,
the curtain finally fall,
in a suspected shower of snowflakes,
with the year going to its death,
fully prepared at every point,
the remaining characters on stage
neither elated, nor surprised,
vanishing into the wings with no regrets,
and no epilogue.

It does not require an audience,
neither approbation, nor disapproval,
and it will finish on time.

But I go under-rehearsed to my death,
I do not know the words by heart,
am uncertain of my cues,
what to expect next,
whether I shall have a second chance
to avoid mistakes at a repeat performance.

Yet I yearn to make myself perfect
who was given Love in full measure,
and power to draw down fire from heaven
at every turn of the year's cycle.

I believe that if I wait in patience,
there will be some late music,
faint sounds of spring breaking in,
and another part to play.
For I know that everything living is holy,
no less in the minute than in the vast,
have still some few moments left
to become a living essence,
still inexperienced and ignorant
but confident in my resurrected being,
warmed at every turn of the year's cycle
by imagination's divine breath.

And so, in this apparent wilderness of winter,
my blind eyes are reopened,
informed by Love, see again,
as I once saw in my innocent childhood,
the first green signs on hedgerows
grass on the move, the hills shining,
and hear the whole earth waking,
creation praising, perfect adoration;
one life in all things.

VOICES

They come again,
those burred voices of my childhood's yesterday;
I hear each one,
sleepless at fevered midnight,
taking me unawares
some snowed hilltop
before the wind takes over.
I am haunted by them,
those insistent voices,
give to each a living face and form,
seeing this one moving
through wet sunlight a country morning,
that one smiling a question mark
when I passed her standing by the long barn.

Why do they speak to me now,
so many cob-webbed years floated away?
Did I make some bargain with them,
have an account to render?
Or is it they beckon me on
where they wait in their whispering shadowland,
as I waited for them
so many times in white fields at harvest,
my head pillowed on corn?

And what they are saying
belongs to another tongue
whose words and grammar I do not know;
I cannot answer them back.

Be silent, then;
I do not want to listen to you,
I feel some guilt I am not with you now,
some remorse I have deserted you.

Have you secrets to share with me,
not revealed when we were together
following the old seasons through?
Let them be.

It will not be long before
I join you where you are.
Be patient. I am not yet ready
to join in your tormenting game.
Let me be,
that I may recall you when I wish,
clothe you with your young flesh.

Do not invade me.

THE HILL

Late larks over Eggardon,
ragwort and scabious blowing,
a few cows streaming homeward;
away on the skyline Atlantic tides flowing
relentlessly over and over the shingle,
early stars showing.

A bland summer evening,
red sun slowly consigning
half of the hill to shadow,
fields on the western slopes to miraculous shining;
soon all will be sombre and silent,
my days declining.

THE WHEAT

I heard its secret whispering,
walking with stars the dewed field path,
a kind of sacramental rustle,
as if at that strange moment created,
acres of burnished corn praising,
bowing down beneath the solemn moon.

A different voice by day,
more familiar and public,
a sun-silvered parade,
every ear laughing, the wind
bending the long lines,
a great clapping of hands.

Night and day,
the shadow of a dark reaper,
silently stalking.

COUNTRY FUNERAL

We buried her, the deadest day that year,
an afternoon of wailing wind and frost,
four young men pushing the old, black bier,
unvarnished coffin, wreathed and crossed.

Thin, broken clouds half-filled the sullen sky,
the feeble sun, a hidden sentinel,
a few shawled women came to say good-bye,
the heavy falling of the mourning bell.

The simple service, then, in fading, thumb-marked books,
"The Resurrection and the Life" its sure belief;
outside the noisy, flapping rooks
in skeleton trees with promise of new leaf.

The family gathered there upon the stiffened grass,
her coffin going down into the chiselled ground,
we saw in retrospect a generation pass,
remembered only by a turf-knit mound.

And left her to her private self in winter's dress;
but soon upon her grave will drop the flying seeds,
with sun to raise them from their nothingness,
and summer grasses for her widow's weeds.

HAWTHORN

I came out into the muted dark
not feeling at one with the lighted room,
suddenly caught the scent of hawthorn flowers,
the night air drenched with it,
there where moon-thick hedges moved up the hill;
the pungency overwhelmed me.

I should have delighted in the strange sweetness,
remembering the thorny thickets of my childhood's forest,
bees plundering the long lines between meadows,
cows and horses nibbling tender crimped leaves,
and how, once, on a fresh May morning,
I plunged my head deep into the clustered flowers,
still moist and shimmering with dew,
and was in ecstasy.

But now, my restless spirit merging with the shadows,
the solemn stillness of that mortal hour,
the hawthorn smelt of death;
and though I had not expected it,
I knew that moment I had seen
my funeral flowers before their time,
breathed the sickly reek of the tomb,
come unprepared to my corruption.

VILLAGE IDIOT

This wind-blown scarecrow flutters with all rags flying
Over open fields, companion of first snow;
Behind him run dancing memories of last night's stars,
Picture of man-in-the-moon upside down in a rocking pool.
Head full of gold wisps and half-forgotten tales,
He would, wind letting, make music to the sky,
Somersault his heart over haystack clouds.
Next year when children come to goggle at him
And then with trembling lip or giggle race away
Into a cuckoo land of hawthorn trees,
He'll range these fields again
Ennobled with daisy crowns, wandering in weed,
Babbling his dictionary of backward words
To his sane self beneath the understanding sun.
He calls no plot of land his own, he cannot write his name,
Yet, lord of toads and master of small birds,
He has angels balancing on needles in his eyes,
And round his skull, heaven's madmen praising God
In secret psalms and songs.

LANDSCAPE

When midwinter bites
rook-haunted meadow and stream,
trees sparkle with frost fire
at the short day's ending,
men come with hunting dogs,
yelping and leashed,
down the white slope of the long hill
turning now to twilight and silver
under early stars.

They trudge mechanically,
warm breaths on rime-seized air
over the stretch of wide fields
where sorted in strawed heaps
gathered roots lie packed face to face
beneath a fortnight's rectangle of solid snow,
past cottage and low-thatched barn
yawning on cobble and square
to the mill's wind-empty arms.

And there
across the iron passageways of the lake
margined by posturing willows,
the village is skating on Martin's Day
with brazier, torch,
bawd, the old country quips,
keeping the feast with bagpipe's revelry.

When night falls on waggon and fold,
grimacing slammerkin, slobbering oaf,
black dogs bay warnings
to the leopards of the moon.

THE SWANS

The winter sky,
Viewed palely through
Branches of poplar, sycamore,
At frosty twilight,
Holds in the watching eye
Leaden silhouettes
Of three swans,
Flapping from the frozen marshes
Where sway drowsy water birds
Underneath shimmering ice spears,
Semi-fractured reeds.

And when night
Falls to cover
The broad sweep of heaven
With legions of stars
Advancing out of cloud mountains,
The swans beat their galleon wings,
Ride the day-remembered air
Still within this room;
Rest comes only when
Their image fades
At the flowering of sleep.

Outside,
Lonely branches grieve,
Whimper through the slow, dark hours,
Forsaken and birdless
Beneath unfriendly skies.

PRISONER

If the dread thing comes, let it come
With nobody to see when his last hour is struck
The passing into darkness of a man
Who once had felt the warmth of gratitude.
And when oblivion stares out of his eyes,
Reason no more lights his brain,
Let the captive stars hang pitying heads
Within the lonely dungeons of the skies
And all their tongues agree to keep in space
Unbroken witness down the years.

ELEMENTS

Words are snow
when silently they drift
into my ears, lodge
along the furrows of the mind,
levelling rough scars,
healing remembered pain,
blotting out bitterness.

And tingling frost
when they crystallise
upon my eyes, flower
unlooked-for in the air,
living, newly formed,
starring the winter sky
with points of brilliance.

Words are ice
when sharp as needles they stab
the patterns of my heart,
agitate its forms;
the ordered sequences
take on a clumsier shape,
have no perfection left
nor innermost design.

ZERO HOUR

Walking Yorkshire lanes
an April morning when the last cold sweat of dew
pearled the budding ends
of blackthorn, elderwood,
moving in patterns of grim agony through the hedge,
I heard over the grass-dank fields,
a solitary lark,
pinioned on high in rocking wonder,
bombing with song on song the pitheads at New Sharleston;
and from a line of new-cut furrows, smarting still
from ploughshare wounds,
the rattle of a battery of warring sparrows
machine-gunning open land at Warmfield.
Unexpectedly I had come upon the eager tumult of spring,
once again my heart turned to battle
that sieged within its armour's pride had thought
    itself impregnable.
Here were sparrow and lark
advancing from the greyness of night's retreat
to make new bridgeheads, fresh vantage points,
in sight of slag-heap and smoke-shocked air;
waste iron sang,
a slime-veiled pond released from barrenness
heaved into greenest pregnancy.

So, like commando birds I shall not retreat,
but stride out from the tunnel of my winter day
over these beds of coal,
bearing no former vision of a man chained
by fetters of confusion,
but armed with pain-forged weapons of attack
strong with resurrection.

MYSTICAL

Neither Plato, nor Galileo,
who worshipped truth,
could have discovered the meaning behind
eye of firecrest or oriole.

Paracelsus,
for all his juggling with stars,
must have started back confounded
at the song which huddled
in the whitethroat's nest.

Loyola split ethical hairs
but held God in his hand
when he balanced on wondering palm
hatching egg of warbler.

NEUTRALITY

Dust on a crumbling page
Blots out the written age,
Greys over what was wise,
Levels truth with lies.

Wind through a hidden crack
Can bring no whistle back
To haunt the caverned mind,
Nor old echoes find.

Speech in silent air
Makes no new fire burn there
When all its barren words
Become like tongueless birds.

When dust and wind and speech
Are mingled each with each,
Love goes down to death,
Hate has no more breath.

WATER MEADOWS

Turn from this sleeping hill
whose blue and jagged edge
has cut the melting link
between earth and sky
to where a spectre fog
has blown abroad his breath,
rolled his steaming beard
across the patchwork plain.
A half-eyed world
within whose acred ease
centuries stand still,
each dew-splintered tree
has silence frail as death.

And now the sun-trapped mist
retreats upon the ridge
to crown again the peaks.
A far-off curlew calls
thin cries upon the wind.
A hidden stream
escaped from boom and tarn
rings clear its pebbled chimes
high over dreaming corn.
The huge theatre of earth
awakes to singing light.

FLOWERS FOR WINTER

Will last the winter through,
these sapless flowers of summer,
colours and forms in a new creation,
stiff grasses not dead,
corn living on, neutral and everlasting;
little stars and stems breathing an immortal air
at the crisp ripeness of the year.

I remember the sun burnishing them,
birds plundering the long furrows,
dew soaking petal and leaf at early morning,
tufted seeds blowing into the wind.

Now let their golden skeletons decorate the house
with all the beauty of their strange architecture,
in shapes and patterns of frail geometry,
challenging the deadness of dark days,
frost on window panes, drear skies;
then in a moment of glad recognition
meet the first flowers of spring again,
as at a resurrection.

THE VALLEY

The long walk through silence nearly over,
suddenly, late afternoon, a hidden valley
I had seen before in dream or vision,
murmuring with the holiness of summer,
a valley of new corn, half-green, half-burnished,
sacramental, everlasting,
huge tides moving towards harvest.
And, recreated at that eternal moment,
I rose with the strong sap, praising,
as the multitude of bending ears praised,
their small voices combining,
swelling with the wind, the valley sounding
a great song of adoration.

I became one with the company of apostles,
for a timeless minute, a saint on earth,
knew the mystery of the miracle of the five loaves,
and Love's fertility.

The sun levelling with earth,
I passed through those shining meadows,
the blessing of dew on mortal shoulders,
the corn still singing,
the whole valley flashing fire,
ringed with archangels.

I heard their trumpets.

VICTIMS

To final ash
break
roots of tortured trees.
Wracked boughs no longer feel
inquisition lash
from forest flames
which now their members seize.
Trees have lost their names,
found the martyrs' stake.
Not one charred leaf
breathes a single prayer,
lifts a voice to make
a gesture of appeal,
a pleading for relief
upon the burning air.

TERROR

The wood is filled
with little frenzied cries
from maddened rushing things
that trapped in grass and fern
in twisted velvet burn
until their whimperings
are meaningless and stilled.

A blazing thrush now sings
with incandescent eyes
as every blackened bird
breaks out from bush and briar
with scorched and failing wings;
mated with fire
with song are sepulchred.

SEDGEMOOR
6th July, 1685 — 6th July, 1977

A secret, melancholy place
where, this dank summer morning,
fog thins out over green withy beds,
meadows, encircled by deep rines;
there are no birds singing,
hedgerows drip rain-tears.

These soaking acres speak of death,
blood-streaked grasses, the peasant army
deceived in the muddy dark,
that warning pistol shot,
Faversham's horses charging;
graveyard of blighted hopes.
In a few seconds I relive, endure
the ninety minutes of that battle.

I see the routed rebels' ranks broken,
flying the field at dawn,
Monmouth's blue and gold standards
sneaking away to false safety,
the foul butchery, and hear the screams,
five hundred herded in Weston Zoyland church.

The assizes are over, Jeffreys is dust,
this murdered ground hides the old bones,
only a sad silence rules now.

No matter who won or lost,
it is a page or two of minor history,
and history has no pity,
neither condemns nor forgives.

MARSH

Beyond the town, the wild marsh,
colour of evening light,
primeval, desolate,
long dykes unruffled,
reflecting last faint streaks of sun
beneath grey clouds drifting.

Only small sounds now;
distant cuckoo with breaking voice,
partridges whirring low over black land,
a heron at late fishing;
a solitary cow chained to a stake
ignores everything but his half-circle of wet grass;
a vole swims quietly from bank to bank.

Horizons darkening, the scene,
familiar enough, but deceptive;
it oozes the old melancholy of history.
I, the one human, in this quagmire landscape,
feel the menace of its strange seclusion,
enter into its silence.
More than a hint of fear in my bones,
as mist begins to brood over field and water,
I move slowly back to the security of the town,
leave the soggy ground to the night.

But come at first light,
these flat acres wake to another dimension;
mists miraculously part to show
hipped hedges flushed with dew,
all the day's colours coming back;
the whole marsh praising.
Purged of its sinister mystery,
land and water rise with every voice to the sun,
everything united in a great cry of adoration,
plant and creature recreated,
the world's first day again,

every bird singing beneath open skies,
snail and vole emblems of magnificence.

Sun on my shoulder,
fear no longer chilling me,
am remade myself;
in perfect unison with nature,
it seems that someone has touched the waters,
breathed a blessing over the land;
I am no longer a solitary.

Surely a vision of holiness,
revealed to me a brief space in time,
yet out of time, in far eternity.
At any moment now
should see a ladder of angels
linking earth and sky,
some small patch shining in Eden.

Until from some high nowhere,
a hawk suddenly dives down,
pins a quivering mouse
in a pool of blood and fur,
mounts up again in triumph,
lost in the pitiless eye of the sun.

BIRDLIP MIRROR

That green Victorian morning on the Crickley road,
he went out only to cut stone,
Joseph Barnfield, Cotswold quarryman;
opened up history.

Three graves in a line,
with bones, feet to the south,
a silver-gilt brooch, rings and bowls,
necklet of amber and jet beads,
and a bronze mirror, unique and delicate;
the Celtic dead unceremoniously brought back
a few dusty moments,
rib-cages suddenly revealed,
skulls bared to the impassive sky.

And one, a woman of the Dobunni tribe,
lovely once, supple as hazel-twig,
dark eyes flashing to the stars,
comely, desirable, kneeling to the sun,
combing her dew-washed hair.

I imagine her admiring smooth skin, proud lips,
in this bright mirror-plate,
new with pounced ornaments, red enamel,
the firm hand of the scriber.

I have known that queen's face in dream,
and see it now, as she saw it,
those dying Roman days,
the strong hills peeping behind her,
shadowed slopes reflected,
the timelessness of unbroken sleep.

The peaks remain unconquered,
valleys are all heather and sheep,
her thin remembering mirror
burnishes this quiet museum room;

I hear her alien laughter still
echoing down the long summer nights,
the moon rising to the full.

And keep my wordless tryst with her.

CIDER-HOUSE

The farmer died fifty years ago,
no child to follow him, the family name
remembered only on a lichened line of gravestones,
one on the war memorial in the north aisle;
the weeds inherited, mildew in the long barn,
bats dangling from rotting beams, blackened ricks,
holes in the thatched shippen,
stars shining through.

New tenants came with silos, tractors,
doubled the cows in the valley meadows,
ten score of sheep balanced on the hills;
left the cider-house empty.
Mice scuttle now through cobweb and moonbeam
where once the little engine purred October mornings away,
the air half-drugged with sweet fumes,
the cutter rusted, the press shrunken and dry.

Only a few remember the cider days,
the shuffle of clogged feet on the littered floor,
fruit piled high in the round baskets,
trundled in from the warm harvesting,
the nodding horses waiting patiently by the orchard gate,
waggons bumping along the ruts to the cool house.

And then all day the golden liquid
trickling, bubble and drop, through the creaking wood,
the engine still humming the same, soft song,
pipes, hogsheads and puncheons filled to the bung,
the raw juice heady, overflowing,
mashed straw and pulp thrown to the pigs.

They are gone now, cider-house and orchards,
the billowing tides of blossoms riding the slopes,
with early bees raiding, and Severn, a silver eel,
twisting to the sea on the far-away skyline.

The magical names remain,
those old apples of cidered Gloucestershire,
Skyrmes Kernel, Dymock Red, and Forest Styre,
Black Foxwhelps and Redstreak;
such honeyed sounds,
pure English poetry in my country ears.
I say each one to myself now, lovely on my tongue,
as ripe and rounded as cider itself,
drunk with long memories from a china mug,
the fire glowing on a winter evening.

ON THE BORDER

A farmstead in Schleswig-Holstein,
ten miles from the frowning border
where wall and mine keep out stranger,
and no birds sing,
house and barn secure in their peace.
An island of freedom at the top of a hill,
it has known no more history
than the small drama of turnips, hay and cabbages,
a few fields of corn, planted and gathered in
from generation to generation,
the land obeying the weather of the seasons,
unbroken patterns from seed-time to harvest,
children at one with the animals
huddled together in sty and milking shed,
the German tongue sounding.

At this soft hour, a summer afternoon,
the farm dreaming the silence of swallows
cascading from shadowy eaves,
butterflies moving their colours from thistle to thistle,
I breathe its holiness,
the wall receding by a hundred miles.

It is a place informed by love,
love unspoken, as lovers speak it,
gentle as rainwater,
cares and conspiracies dropping away,
a community waking to the sun,
going its slow, untroubled way until the moon
rises in mystery above the trees;
there is something here I only apprehend,
something deeper than silence.

And walking your glowing acres,
I was so close to you in your remoteness
it seemed I had escaped from an alien existence,
a deathly territory of wire and wall,

inherited another dimension,
the long perspective of clockless time
you chose for your journeyings.
And could have stayed with you for this,
following your simple rule with my love,
year after year, the German tongue sounding,
until, flesh and bone crumbling,
I became a minute particle of your dynamic earth,
giving back what you gave,
a few small blades of living grass.

BIOLOGICAL EXPERIMENT

A dead frog cannot be quickened into being,
renew the trembling and battle of creation
along the quadrant of his limbs;
the current to do this would have to come
from a dynamo, not from a small volt battery.

Yet, somewhere, there must be a needle,
pregnant and sharp enough,
to push into the frog's faint beating muscles
and waken them, if only in holiday mood,
into some bitter kind of idiocy.

The marsh with its foulness waits, the rushes
claim the last communion of its broken body;
one would need the accumulated energy of a million power
    stations
working against time, to bring back the shape,
the old pattern of its breathing.

Too late now, or too soon;
this bottled frog has become an insignificant part
of the waste of frustration,
which, in itself, is indestructible.

DELIVERY

She watches the last push, the hard work over,
the midwife waiting there,
unruffled in her white patience,
for the nameless one to come out into the light.

Secure in her confidence she controls the crowning head,
a beautiful and wonderful revelation,
sees the moist, corkscrew hair,
the mother panting, beaded with sweat.

The little black baby emerges,
eyes closed as it slides forward,
the moulded head rotating a circle's quarter;
she wipes the eyes, and then, with deft, remembering hands,
eases out each slippery shoulder.

The rest of him comes easily enough.

Now he is on his own, this manikin,
ready to be presented to a face of smiles,
the miracle complete, nature fulfilled.
In a few moments he has inherited his home,
a unique and perfect being,
a gift worth waiting for.

It is a normal birth.

But hidden deep in him,
the whimpering sounds of far-off western isles
floating with palm trees in a coral sea,
and deeper still,
what weeping memories of the sugar plantations,
Africa burning, the slavers' lash,
and new-born babies dying in foul holds?

He has come from that old agony to this.

STILL BORN

I carried you in hope,
the long nine months of my term,
remembered that close hour when we made you,
often felt you kick and move
as slowly you grew within me,
wondered what you would look like
when your wet head emerged,
girl or boy, and at what glad moment
I should hear your birth cry,
and I welcoming you
with all you needed of warmth and food;
we had a home waiting for you.

After my strong labourings,
sweat cold on my limbs,
my small cries merging with the summer air,
you came. You did not cry.
You did not breathe.
We had not expected this;
it seems your birth had no meaning,
or had you rejected us?

They will say that you did not live,
register you as still born.
But you lived for me all that time
in the dark chamber of my womb;
and when I think of you now,
perfect in your little death,
I know that for me you are born still;
I shall carry you with me for ever,
my child, you were always mine,
you are mine now.

Death and life are the same mysteries.

DEAF AND DUMB

Cannot hear birds, wind in trees,
small field noises,
thunder of brooks at flood time,
sighs, echoes,
or any music;
I groan in my throat like a beast,
eager to praise with my mute tongue.
Yet know, by touch, heart of stone,
hair like wire on moth's back,
knife-edge of grass,
death in an autumn leaf.
And see what you do not see,
details you miss at casual glance,
strange flower in ruined garden,
pad of fox, first corn shoot,
the wordless look.
Can only come to you
where you talk in closed companies
when eyes speak, a finger beckons.
Then, reading your lips,
I walk unchained on soundless feet,
wait in the shadows for tears to fall,
huge as waterfalls,
on your dumb hands,
my deaf ears.

MONGOL

No little monster lumbering through your door,
for all my floppy muscles, lolloping tongue,
so do not be put off by how I look;
I know how you shudder when you see
my slanting eyes, low-set ears,
thanking your lucky stars you are not like me.
You look strange to me.

I am a loving creature,
would put my arms around you
if I did not feel you recoil,
happy with a simple life you have forgotten,
singing and talking to myself the day long
in a world you do not inhabit;
we are all princes in our dominion.

I cannot always cope,
have to rely on you for so much.
Accept me, then. I have accepted you;
I am different, that is all,
as nightingales are from eagles.
How secure are you in your normality?

Look at me now where I grin foolishly at you;
I did not choose to be like this,
but can talk, jump, use my hands,
learn to do many things,
can be a good and willing worker.

I shall never produce my facsimile,
so, if you are disappointed in me,
be grateful for that.

You could, of course, have destroyed me
before I was born;
I am grateful you did not.

THE BIRTHS

Coming in from the fields,
all night under stars,
ewes at their full time,
he brings the sharp morning with him,
frost on his shoulder,
carrying snug under flapping coat
a lamb born in the half-light,
weak and breathing warm
into the welcoming house.

Seven o'clock air nipping his fingers,
cows bellowing in the dark byre,
he hears from upstairs room
glad and sudden birth-cry,
his first child delivered at that chill hour
coming in from the fields;
with proud eyes greets mother and son,
peaceful after strugglings,
lays the lamb at their feet,
wordless, leaves them to the mystery.

At the kitchen table ponders the coincidence,
child and lamb arriving together,
new life inheriting the old meadows,
the farm waking to soft flurries of snow
coming in from the fields,
a far bird calling,
spring knocking on the womb of winter.

MASTER OF THE CHORISTERS

The tablet on the flaking wall,
sun-dappled south aisle, Exeter Cathedral,
could be passed by. Hard to believe
"Matthew Godwin, Mus. B. Oxon,
Master of the Music, Canterbury and Exeter,
died 1586, aged 17."

Little else known of him,
no music by Godwin remains,
no writing or portrait,
but at 15 years, this child became,
a Canterbury chapter minute records,
organist and master of the children;
his degree, too, is registered,
college unknown.

Only a few months at Exeter,
then the final cadence,
snatched abruptly into the tomb,
his music over.

Are tears needed now?
The heart is moved to them.
So young for genius to be born in him,
then, so suddenly silenced by the dark,
promise barely fulfilled.
Too old for his years?
Too soon a flowering?
Futile speculations;
the few facts, though, haunt and trouble.

But sometimes at winter Evensong,
Exeter and Canterbury, snow falling,
it seems his requiem is still sung,
the ruffed children sending to the stars
the old Tudor counterpoint,
Gibbons, Mundy, Batten and Byrd,
anthems by Tallis and Tye.

Little master, I must not grieve;
you brought the music with you,
carried it back from whence it came.
Hark, child, your tablet is rejoicing here,
the words are on fire and singing
a Te Deum for your 17 years,
the Resurrection and the Life.

LATE OF THIS PARISH

They buried him by the long wall,
primroses at feet and head,
this villager, scholar, priest,
an afternoon of rainbowed showers,
cuckoos calling in the near copse,
commenting on the final scene;
last vicar of this parish.

More than thirty years of sermons,
watching the shadows fall with memories
on the growing lines of gravestones,
the great yew tree shading him now,
christenings, marriages, funerals,
the parish rounds, farms and cottages.

A simple man for all his learning,
not easily confounded by secular argument;
brave in adversity,
changing fashion did not change him,
for ever faithful to the old prayer book,
his daily office, the church's calendar,
a comfort to the sick in mind or body;
did not fawn to archdeacons and bishops.

The moles now work over and under him,
the rambling vicarage empty but for remembering footfalls,
the garden in ruin, children scattered;
but the bells he often rang in the grey tower
still circling his name,
writing his epitaph on the wind;
and something for ever in this breathing churchyard
which cannot be defined,
but is alive, immense, though out of time.

VISIT TO EDMUND BLUNDEN

An afternoon in September,
hedges gone crazy with the last of summer,
I came through stubbled cornfields,
a final pilgrimage, perhaps, to the old poet,
suddenly between clumped trees,
the great tower of Long Melford church,
then the millhouse, sleeping by the muffled stream.

At first he did not know me,
where he sat, florid, white-haired,
upright at the kitchen table,
the day's newspaper unread,
the customary glass of beer half-drunk,
until, my hand on his thickening shoulder,
he smiled a welcome, and said my name,
the minutes and motes floating over us;
only that once did he speak,
the rest, far away, almost anonymous.

I thought of the man he once was,
the fine handwriting, the scholarship,
the poems he had written of English fields and rivers,
remembered the soft country voice
talking about cricket, trench warfare;
all gone now. The past, oblivion,
the future, a sea of vacancy.

Sun stroking the garden,
the calf-bound books forgotten on their shelves,
I walked away into a rainbow shower,
tears, it seemed, from infinity,
leaving him behind, calm and motionless,
happy in the tomb of his silence,
wearing the death mask of Clare.

FOR A CHRISTENING

Welcome to earth, child,
bring the new life with you;
we are waiting for you here with our light,
the morning and evening stars singing together,
every grass blade, frost flower, field creature,
praising at this holy midwinter hour,
earth in unison with heaven.

You chose us to receive you,
we open the windows of our love to you,
that in your fragility you may come in;
we place our hands in your hands.
The water, salt and ash are offered,
infinite, sacramental;
water for life,
salt for form,
ash, the seed of the future spirit,
consecrated in the rainbow of the Trinity.

And so you are born again,
you have a name and an abiding place,
we are all your family,
a community of living,
one with the eternal Christ,
complete and sanctified.

Beautiful and strange that you should come,
softly as the snow comes, on Christmas night,
as long ago He came to the strawed stable,
mother, father, animals watching over,
as now we keep our vigil over you,
watchers and witnesses;
birth's agony over, the long journey before you,
the future still to be created,
mystery on mystery,
the baptismal light still following.

EARLY PORTRAIT

A country boy,
exiled now in London, bred in Gloucestershire
where Severn flows serenely, the white cathedral tower,
a secure and Norman landmark beneath Cotswold skies.
Brought up among trees, Forest of Dean,
coal mines glimpsed over heads of foxgloves;
wandered, a dreamer, bluebelled glades all hours, day and night,
knew where foxes hid, once saw a golden eagle;
sang with small but true voice in the church choir, no angel,
with corn-coloured curls could have been mistaken for one,
stocky, sharp-eyed, a fleet runner, eager to please,
very vulnerable, easily brought to tears;
played village cricket, did not excel,
outgoing by nature, knew many gypsies, tramps,
often in trouble, plagued my mother and teachers,
eyed girls nervously, too shy to approach one.
At Monmouth school, scholarship boy, but poor,
learned the Latin tongue, little French, no mathematics,
a rough and cunning rugby player;
an odd mixture, loved music, poetry,
all strange and rural things, the changing seasons,
had green fingers, an eager, bespectacled reader.

Knew sorrow, disappointment, never hunger,
had perfect health, not easily daunted,
stumbled along somehow, my childhood days,
guided by some light glowing within me,
never lost a sense of wonder.

Aware now though of mistakes I made,
my hot temper and impatience,
grateful for good fortune, home and friends,
loyal to their memory, count my blessings,
looking calmly into the future,
a country boy still,
exiled now in London.

MAURICE

He reads the weather in the country signs,
printed, dawn and dusk, on wooded hills,
the changing face of stream and sky;
hears all the village news on his private wind,
takes it around with him, fair or foul,
sharing it with friends who gladly come
to greet him in his favourite, welcoming inn,
enjoying the pleasure of his jovial company.

A gentle man, no cynicism in him,
his help is freely given, early or late,
his head so full of enterprises and schemes
that, carol singing over, summer's fête begins;
haymaking to harvest the meadows know him.

As innocent as the daisies, new and white,
which star the churchyard turf in spring,
and, where, one day the news will be
that he has joined the lines of those who knew his worth;
the sun shall bless him, the remembering rain
not wash away the simple record of his deeds.

He will lie there in peace, at home,
bell sounds floating high over him,
bees murmuring on the wing,
grasses waving his name,
the young trout rising.

RECTOR

Would have been at home in any century,
this good-humoured priest, adapted well to each;
natural qualities include patience,
ability to spot the counterfeit,
courage to condemn it.

Think of him in the late eighteenth,
going the parish rounds, country or city church,
scholar's hood worn lightly, bands and wig,
preaching the word, comforting the sick,
sitting late at night in candle-lit study,
honouring the Book of Common Prayer;
of the faithful company of Donne and Herbert,
but affinities, too, with the English mystics;
would have been acceptable, without a doubt,
at Parson Woodforde's dinner table;
has a fund of anecdotes.

Enough of the visionary in him to see angels
walking through Smithfield at their ease,
enough of the evangelical to raise no alarm
at York or Canterbury, a Broad Churchman,
lodged happily here for forty years
with Norman pillars, arches and aisles;
a perfect musical setting.

For all his knowledge of theology,
there is a heart beating warm beneath that red cassock,
and a rebel struggling to break out in fury
against the machinations of systems and hierarchies;
and has done so on occasions.

Rahere, of course, knows most about him,
and will speak in due time.

VIRGER

The small procession over, the silver cross
fixed and glittering in the lanterned stalls,
the visiting preacher pokered to his place,
a late worshipper welcomed in whispers,
he hurries down the south aisle on quiet feet,
past black memorial tablets,
grave monuments in their marbled silence,
is hidden for a second or so by the Norman pillars;
then disappears, a monastic ghost, into the shadows,
will not be seen again until sermon time,
to switch off lights, the church in half-darkness,
only the tall candles burning in steady prayer
on the flowered altar, the founder's tomb.

Oblate of Nashdom, he has the liturgy by heart,
a gentle, forgiving man, will defend the Catholic faith
against all comers, knows his own mind;
loves the mystery of the Mass, blessing of bread and wine,
longs to see a censer swinging, the smoke rising.

His natural place, this shrine,
where Augustinians once sang their plain-chant offices
from frost-cold Lauds to chillier Compline,
he keeps faith with the old dispensation.

Evensong come to its soft close,
the dim nave still full of praising witnesses,
he ponders over the coming week,
the same daily round,
weddings, christening, funerals,
more polishing in the Lady Chapel,
the stone Cloister floor to be scrubbed,
and visitors to be shown round.

The long line of dead abbots approve,
smile benevolently from their watching window.

RETROSPECT OF ANDREW YOUNG

His head full of wild flowers,
their names and habitats,
memories of mountains, the old poets,
he walked the world in solid silence
as if out of tune with it,
but eyes and ears missing nothing,
rare plant on meadow path, seashore,
bird skulking in misty hedgerow,
a visionary, pondering on heaven and hell,
earth's mysteries and contradictions;
his knowledge was formidable.

Few words though, did not seem to need them,
poems honed to sharpest bone,
compressed to the smallest compass of wonder.

Could have been mistaken for a farmer,
this dour priest, up in London for the day,
a face chiselled out of biblical rock,
yet with a vein of quicksilver,
waiting to surprise at any moment,
challenging, confounding.

I see him now on some barrowed hilltop,
clouds rolling parables over him,
fingering a frosted arrowhead,
history binding him to the hand that carved it,
hear him solemnly preaching to his flock,
a Harvest Sunday, the far fields shining,
the wheat immortal, everlasting,
poems shaping themselves slowly within him,
seed by seed.

LISTENING AND TRAVELLING

de la Mare? I knew him well,
that old poet of visionary loveliness,
remember how he looked at me, probingly,
from dark, kind eyes, taking my hand,
the words he spoke of mystery and wonder
as if Somebody beyond was listening.
He was a gentle man, no stiffness or rancour,
passionate about children, the world's injustices,
his warm spirit searching for reality,
catching its gleam in flower and bird,
shine on snow, sea shores and water meadows,
and all the small phenomena of common day.

Haunted by presences in the dark shades,
evil decked up in clothes of innocence,
did not deceive himself, recoil from their menace.
Hungry for truth asked unanswerable questions,
intrigued more with "Why?" than with "How?";
once said his poems were visitors
making some of them stay for ever.

I see him now moving about the Twickenham house
leaning on walking stick, breath short, smiling still,
a Listener longing for the eternal hour,
his own Traveller, Eden his home.

Yes, I remember him well, and hear him now
calling me to walk in fields of asphodel,
beckoning me to sundown and dewfall in the lost Hesperides.

SERMONS IN STONES

Long dead to village gossip and lies,
the Reverend Samuel Wallis, Master of Arts,
Vicar of Loders and Bradpole, 1820—1835,
buried here, a grey stone slab in the choir,
"With Molly, his wife";
no other details.

There was whispering and scandal enough,
all the commandments broken, a self-righteous age,
when Samuel ranged these parish fields,
visiting the sick, the tardy church-goer,
the same lies told, the same calumny;
men and women do not change
whatever monarch or weather rules.

And did he close his ears,
bury himself alive in classical studies,
the vicarage fires comfortably burning?
Pray for lost souls on threadbare knees?
Or thunder forth iniquities,
lumping sinners and saved together?
And all without profit.

We shall never know,
there are no records of him,
the kind of man he was,
lion or lamb;
it has no consequence.

A particle of dust now,
Samuel Wallis is floating freely in Dorset air,
his ministry forgotten.

The chattering tongues live on.

STEDMAN

So little known of him,
Fabian Stedman, printer and bell-ringer;
born Cambridge, 1631, in a time of plague,
the parish registers do not record him;
College Youth Master at his half-century,
he printed the new peals
on casual slips of rough paper,
published his little book "Tintinnalogia";
nothing else is certain,
the mists of history have hidden him.

His name lives on,
solid and foursquare as a page of Tallis,
called out every day of the year
some ringing room or other, country and town;
his method has given him immortality,
the well-struck changes ringing out their music,
doubles, triples and caters,
the bells obeying his clear mathematics,
ringers concentrating and contemplative;
such sounds, mellow and fresh,
as on the first day Stedman was rung
almost anonymously at St. Benet's church,
making their smooth way from rounds to rounds.

An English genius,
of the company of Shakespeare and Constable,
his fame falling surely at this evensong moment
on Thames flowing serenely with swans past St. Paul's,
Stedman Cinques decorating the calm Sunday air,
the bells gloriously swinging,
prayer and praise floating to the flashing stars,
Southwark challenging on the other side.

NOTHING LOST

Their heads full of Stedman and Grandsire,
they toppled over into country graves,
those eager bellringers of yesterday,
mouldering now beneath simple mounds
raised on the anonymous turf,
not far from the lichened tower,
taking the ordered sounds they lived with
into death's silence.

They walked in from the villages around,
practice nights and Sundays,
men from forge and farm,
to join the rector in long cassock
who rang with them before service began;
the doctor's son came, the gardener from the big house,
postman, schoolmaster and stonemason.
They were at one with the bells,
pulling away methodically, matins and evensong,
bound to the habit.

All gone now, but nothing is lost,
the sounds are still there in the listening air.

And when at the resurrection they meet again,
Stedman and Grandsire will come easily enough,
and they, reunited in the ringing room,
perfectly at home with rope and sally,
dodge and hunt, the quick rounds repeated,
men and bells clamouring to speak the old praises,
incorruptible.

BELLRINGERS

Meet in secret companies,
church towers, bar parlours,
from all professions and trades;
there are no class barriers.
Almost anonymous, few seem to know of their existence,
what they do when not pulling bells.

Thousands of them,
men, women and children scattered over the countries,
ringing the changes a few hours weekly,
cities and old villages;
it has been like this for centuries.
Like gipsies and bees they are great travellers,
every ringing chamber welcomes them;
their knowledge of geography is considerable.

A curious fraternity with a common language
they practise an ancient mystery,
handed down to them, year in, year out,
by word of mouth and example,
learning from the older ringers
how to control bells with confidence,
striking well, raising and lowering them,
making bobs or singles when they are called,
mastering the methods
until Stedman and Grandsire are in their bones.

Priding themselves on accuracy,
they watch their neighbours during peals
like cats watch mice;
very English, are companions of silence in sombre circles,
tongues only unloosed when talking of their craft.

And do they realise when ringing,
the bells are sending their prayers to heaven,
the methods are little sermons in sound,
touches of holiness?

SUNDAY

In Cumbria they are ringing minimus at Lazonby,
four bells, too, on the go at Muggington in Derby,
Grandsire Doubles at Holy Cross, Ashton Keynes,
the twelve-hundredweight tenor with a lovely tone;
the light bells at St. Bartholomew-the-Great,
    oldest in London,
calling the people anti-clockwise to Evensong,
a perfect quarter peal of Bob Doubles with any luck.

Down at Westbury-on-Severn in Gloucestershire,
Severn sparkling only half a mile away,
the six ringers are tackling an extent of Stedman Doubles
in the detached tower of St. Mary-the-Virgin;
and at Loders, Dorset men and women,
are improving their call changes, the tower captain
just able to cope with the nineteen-hundredweight tenor
when they pull the bells up.

Triples at St. Keverne in Cornwall, Wigton in
    Leicestershire,
full bands turned up today, a few visitors
asking questions about the art and mystery;
the nine bells at All Saints, Basingstoke, are hard at it,
proud of their uniqueness, have a long history;
Shrewsbury St. Mary rang 5219 caters in 1811,
3 hours 25 minutes, Mr. William Bull calling,
now they may be flooding the town with Oxford Treble
    Bob Royal,
while at Wells Cathedral, the moated swans are listening,
the choir is all ready in the stalls.

Ringers at Accrington St. James in fine form, a light
    tenor here,
the bells at Great Yarmouth St. Nicholas,
largest parish church in England,
can be heard far out at sea,
a good touch of cinques.

All over England today, every county,
village, city, bells praising,
summoning the people to worship, morning, evening,
an unbroken rising and falling of prayer.

NO RINGER

Came to bellringing late in life,
failed to learn the art,
though yearned to do so.
For all my patient teacher's skill,
I often panicked when, with fluttering heart,
hung on too long at handstroke,
or missed the sally,
looking for it to come down,
I saw myself carried up with the swing,
the bell maddened and breaking the stay,
or crashing down in vengeance on my head.

I did not have the temperament,
fearful imagination blocked my way,
to give me feel of balance, full control;
I should have done better in my 'teens.

They said my stance was right,
my arms were never bent,
they knew I longed to learn,
encouraged me with kind words,
saying that it would come.
It never did.

Defeated, I retired, sat by the wall,
watching the others pull away
as if it were their second nature;
I envied them.

No mathematician, nor did I need
the mental challenge, but just loved
the ancient music of the bells,
and names of all the changes,
Singles and Bobs, Doubles, Caters,
Minimus, Royals and Cinques;
English poetry sounding in English air.
Knew what a Hunt was, and a Dodge,

could follow through the courses,
enjoyed the company of ringers in many towers.

My consolation is I go to sleep
with some old village church clear in my eye,
close wrapped in snow at Christmas time,
and hear its bells, mellow across the fields,
a city ringing room in summer
hailing a royal wedding, beginning of a reign.

My hope that, at my end,
the bells will ring for me, a muffled peal,
before, the hushed echoes fading,
they lay me to rest in a country grave,
a man who rejoiced in bells,
but could not do the thing itself.

Maybe, in heaven, the power will be granted me,
so that I ring at perfect ease
with Stedman, Shipway and Troyte,
and hosts of simple ringers,
touches of Grandsire Triples,
crisp sets of Cambridge Surprise.

FATHOM FIVE

The stream has found its mouth
and tide of satisfaction;
Here its waters stay
In calm-anointed strength
Alone and isolated.
We sail on into wide white seas
For further visitations,
Born strange and high
On waves of bewilderment
Out and beyond the range
Of former voices
Into the seas wide and white with new meaning.
Out and beyond the beam
Winking faintly over the harbour
The grief of drowned seamen
Who in coral and bone
Remember no charts
Nor the day of their foundering.

SCALABER BECK

Break, then, heart,
in this predestined place
where river, rock,
remember no face,
nor tangle of weeds
give back the shock,
the limb-blunted sound
of new death
when black waters part.
Finger no beads;
this is old burial ground.
Echoes of sudden-stopped breath
emptied on limitless air,
dissolved in a dream
of owl-dimming light,
never more bruised upon stone.
Stifle any prayer,
let the tongues of this stream
cleft in their pain
run mute in the night,
that one bird grieving alone
be silent again.

SILENCES

When by harsh circumstance parted from you,
they come back to me in sleep and dream,
those old woods of my childhood,
snow-hung and solemn in midwinter,
new birds shrilling at budding-time,
I remember how I walked in them,
all hours of night and day, a solitary,
eyes missing nothing, ears receiving
every faint sound falling on leafy air,
pondering a mystery I felt deeply,
could not fathom because of innocence,
in that ocean of stillness.

I know now that in my young melancholy
I was waiting for you to be born,
that you were somewhere there, out of time,
part of the silence of those trees,
a created spirit, not yet conceived,
speaking your peace to my spirit as I moved
restlessly between high banks of fern,
pigeons mourning above me,
sun breaking through high branches.

And now imprisoned in my solitude,
I reach out again for you, believing
that if I could take you back with me,
even at this late hour,
into the heart of those calm woods,
we should find the meaning of the mystery
that troubled me, needing no words,
nor blink of an eyelid,
touch of a finger, to explain it,
but hearing once again far-off echoes of our eternity,
as we heard them together in the long ago,
one spirit breathing in those living silences,
immortal, indivisible.

EXILES

And one shall then return,
though two shall come
upon the morning tide.

And one shall stay and learn,
in grief's millenium
the fruits of pride.

And one shall storm the wave
to seek another light
beyond the looming reef.

And one shall find a grave,
and there marooned in night
strike seams of new belief.

VALLEY OF SHADOW

Where the path begins to turn through the darkening valley,
Bare mountains on either side rising with silent mourning,
We came in our anguish, the brief journey in time almost over,
One to go forward, both to turn round, look back and seeing
                Hands waving farewell.

Never to meet on earth again, delivered like Ishmaels to our
    wanderings,
An end of sharing all we had made, all we believed in,
The sun going down in a haze of blood, our cold long shadows,
Such a small space of time but years ahead for remembering
                Eyes weeping farewell.

Yet something precious remains, more than a frail dream of
    memories,
The future unknown, there may be nothing beyond this dim
    valley
But a dead land of rocks, no green fields or rivers,
A few faint sounds echoing on the hilltops, we for ever hearing
                Voices saying farewell.

Now to the final minute together, the vision of beauty slow
    fading,
Hands, eyes and voices combined can no longer bring any
    consoling,
We know what is moving within us, that Love will never be
    broken;
Let the night fall on all things as now we are both feeling
                Hearts beating farewell.

THE WAY IT WAS

They all knew, but said nothing,
those watching ones, company of friends,
standing still and impassive there;
an open secret, they showed no signs
that Love was breathing in that place
where bells sang, soft light fell.
The two did not look at each other
but, darting shy glances at the calm faces,
wondered if in their courtesy they guessed
the way it was with them;
for all their agreed discretion,
their innocence gave the game away;
lovers' eyes do not lie.
The others were happy for them,
sharing the unsaid rapture of their joy.
Even when the two slipped away,
the ringing over, into the muffled dark,
the others remained faithful,
kept their pact of delicate silence,
smiled wisely, talked of other things.
Such was the nature of their pure acceptance,
clear recognition without comment,
a true relationship understood,
needing no analysis.

And they together, alone with their mystery,
inheriting a common kingdom,
held hands like children,
the night enfolding them,
so transfigured they said nothing.

VIGIL

I said the binding word,
must keep my vigil now
where winter's voice is heard
shouting through bush and bough,
the dead lie sepulchred.

Who looked for final grace
before their last farewell
and in this resting place
no longer fear the bell
but fill so small a space.

Where now alone I kneel
their binding words were said
and every grief I feel
felt once by these old dead
whose wounds refuse to heal.

Wounds that I must bear
as if each one was mine
become this vigil's prayer;
it is their bread and wine
which at this hour I share.

And with the nightwatch gone
I walk into the light
which round their heads once shone
as holy and as bright
as fire in Babylon.

THE SOUNDING OF THE HORN

At the sounding of the horn
I believe that we shall see
every field of harvest corn
more golden in eternity.

And the end of anger's strife,
peace as on its first day's birth,
and the waking of new life
in the common grains of earth.

Could we not be sometimes touched
by the tongues of heavenly fire,
who so often have been smutched
by the blots of false desire?

And, believing, learn to trace
what is there for all to find,
blessings on the water's face,
healing for the inly blind?

Free as birds at morning light
we can move in visionary air,
and, in wonder, catch a sight
of the opening flowers at prayer.

Listen to the breathing stones
and the secret songs they sing;
in each heap of powdered bones
beats the sound of distant wings.

At the sounding of the horn
when the final bell is tolled,
every element reborn,
every mystery unfold.

CHRISTE, CHRISTE

Evensong over,
the music brought to its final cadence,
the door to the cloister closes.
The last voices die away,
merging with the last footfall into muffled silence;
the church is empty now,
no echoes whispering in the darkness.

Not empty, though.
There are other footfalls, other voices,
the old brothers assembling in black-cowled lines,
the cloister door opening,
moving along the cold aisles into the candled choir,
Rahere listening from his new tomb,
waiting in his dust for the Mass to begin.
        Kyrie Eleison,
        Christe, Christe, eleison.

Everything alive here,
men with angels praising,
Heaven receiving.
        Gloria in excelsis Deo
        et in terra pax hominibus.

Think sometimes, then,
Time cancelled out,
this night, every night,
evensongs over,
how Eternity continues to loom here,
and Love lifted up again.
        Qui tollis peccata mundi,
        miserere nobis.

Tomorrow will break on Lauds,
the same ghostly company,
the waking City.
        Benedictus qui venit in nomine Domini.

BENEDICTION

Walking with sunlight the early morning,
the City streets in their day's infancy,
rain spotted down, a brief shower,
anointing, for a miraculous moment, head and eyes,
healing the mind of the night's tremors;
it was a blessing.

Then, in the cool of the long afternoon,
walking at peace the old churchyard garden,
crumbling headstones, anonymous names
once of this parish, a masquerade of wallflowers
perfuming dead and living,
a spider wove his wonder, perfect geometry,
a bee claimed all the territory of the dappled turf;
it was all a blessing.

On knees now beneath the singing arches,
echoes of prayers in choir and cloister,
a time to give thanks for the sacraments of rain and sun,
as outside, dew falls, shadows,
first stars ride the twilight sky.

The altar, a blaze of candles,
the evening office sung,
Body and Blood are displayed;
the blessing of blessings.

PILGRIM

You who casually tread these aisles
all weathers, all seasons,
what are your thoughts, feelings,
as moving round you peer at this and that?
Have you come, by chance or design,
only with curiosity's eye
to collect a few more evidences of old history?

You are a pilgrim
with neither staff nor scallop shell;
but an inner light is guiding you,
your spirit naked to the Presence,
living and burning here.

Contemplate a while
before you take another step;
ask yourself why, and for Whom,
these eloquent arches were raised.
Then thank the Maker,
so that when you cease from gazing,
rejoin what oppresses outside,
you will continue in your contemplation,
discover where the true meaning is.

PRAYER TO GOD THE FATHER

You created me,
placed me, a living creature, on earth,
a person in my own right,
unique, a free spirit.
You breathed into me feeling, imagination,
fixed in me a will to decide for myself,
the unfathomable power of love;
so many gifts of heart and mind,
abundant treasures.

Teach me, then, to be true to myself,
to respect my individuality;
give me wisdom and insight
that I may recognise the individuality of others,
and attend to their needs;
greater understanding, more patience,
that I may have a proper perspective.
And grant me courage enough
to withstand conflict, endure pain,
and never fall into despair.

I know that it is a lot to ask for,
who, so far, have not been much of a compliment to you.

But I also know that you will never abandon me,
your feeble and wayward child,
either in life or death,
that I can always speak to you,
even without words.

Thank you for creating me,
for giving me so much,
and forgive me for failing you so often,
wasting your treasures.

Keep a sense of wonder in me,
an innocence that is not deceived or destroyed;
then I can continue to see perfect images of you
in all your creations,
marvel at their glory and beauty,
and so worship you better,
Who are Perfection,
from Everlasting to Everlasting.

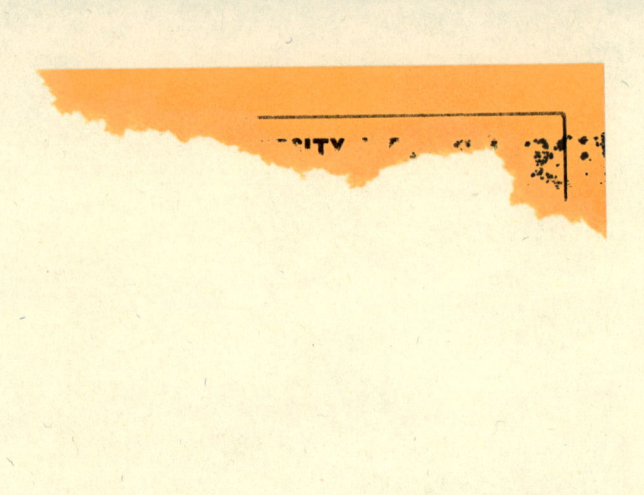